ALSO BY BILLY COLLINS

POETRY

Picnic, Lightning

Sailing Alone Around the Room

Nine Horses

The Trouble with Poetry

Ballistics

Horoscopes for the Dead

Aimless Love

The Rain in Portugal

Whale Day

Musical Tables

Water, Water

ANTHOLOGIES

Poetry 180: A Turning Back to Poetry

180 More: Extraordinary Poems for Every Day

Bright Wings: An Anthology of Poems About Birds

DOG
SHOW

DOG SHOW

Poems

BILLY COLLINS

WATERCOLORS BY PAMELA SZTYBEL

RANDOM HOUSE
NEW YORK

Random House
An imprint and division of Penguin Random House LLC
1745 Broadway, New York, NY 10019
randomhousebooks.com
penguinrandomhouse.com

Hardcover ISBN 978-0-593-97941-9
Ebook ISBN 978-0-593-97942-6

Printed in Canada

9 8 7 6 5 4 3

BOOK TEAM: Production editor: Jennifer Rodriguez • Managing editor: Rebecca Berlant • Production manager: Mark Maguire • Copy editor: Briony Everroad • Proofreaders: Claire Maby, Melissa Churchill

The authorized representative in the EU for product safety and compliance is Penguin Random House Ireland, Morrison Chambers, 32 Nassau Street, Dublin D02 YH68, Ireland. https://eu-contact.penguin.ie.

THIS BOOK IS DEDICATED TO

Addison	Dotty
Adele	Edith
Angus	Elektra
Audrey	Ernie
Aurora	Gide
Bane	Grover
Barry	Holly
Bart	Honey
Bear	Hudson
Beauregard	Idgie
Belle	Jackson
Blue	Jeannine
Bradley	Joey
Bucky	Jonah
Camper	Kennan
Chance	Kenny
Chevy	Lefty
Colonel	Lola
Dapples	Luke

Lydia

Mabel

Maisie

Marcy

Mick

Miles

Mona Lisa Lisa

Morrison

Murphy

Ollie

Nemo

Nico

Paulo

Peanut

Perry

Pip

Preston

Pronto

Radio

Rafer

River Valley Chieftain

Roo

Roxie

Sally

Samus

Sandy

Scrambler

Serena

Simcoe

Skippy

Slick

Sparky

Stanley

Stella

Suzette

Tremor

Trigger

Tux

Venus

Wagner

Wags

Wally

Walter

Willie

Winnie

Winry

Zeke

*"God . . . sat down for a moment when the dog
was finished in order to watch it . . . and to know
that it was good, that nothing was lacking, that
it could not have been made better."*

—RILKE

CONTENTS

DOG
SHOW

DHARMA

The way the dog trots out the front door
every morning
without a hat or an umbrella,
without any money
or the keys to her dog house
never fails to fill the saucer of my heart
with milky admiration.

Who provides a finer example
of a life without encumbrance—
Thoreau in his curtainless hut
with a single plate, a single spoon?
Gandhi with his staff and his wire spectacles?

Off she goes into the material world
with nothing but her brown coat
and her modest blue collar,
following only her wet nose,
the twin portals of her steady breathing,
followed only by the plume of her tail.

If only she did not shove the cat aside
every morning
and eat all his food
what a model of self-containment she would be,
what a paragon of earthly detachment.
If only she were not so eager
for a rub behind the ears,
so acrobatic in her welcomes,
if only I were not her god.

WEIGHING THE DOG

It is awkward for me and bewildering for him
as I cradle him in my arms
balancing our weight on the bathroom scale,

but this is the way to weigh a dog, and easier
than training him to sit obediently in one spot
with his tongue out, waiting for the cookie.

With pencil and paper, I subtract my weight
from our total to find out the remainder that is his,
and I start to wonder if there is an analogy here.

It could not have to do with my leaving you,
though I never figured out what you amounted to
until I subtracted myself from our combination.

You held me in your arms more than I held you
through all those awkward and bewildering months
and now we are both lost in strange and distant neighborhoods.

IN PRAISE OF IGNORANCE

On a bench one afternoon
in a grassy park in Minneapolis,
I realized what I liked best
about the dogs of Minneapolis
is that they have no idea they're in Minneapolis.

The same could be said
of the dogs of Houston or Philadelphia,
it occurred to me on the slow walk
back to my hotel, but I was
in no mood to be distracted.

I'm sticking with the dogs of Minneapolis,
I resolved, as the elevator
rose to my floor, just as they stick
with their owners, the natives of Minneapolis,
most of whom know exactly where they are.

Then I stood on the 17th floor,
surveying the vast prospect below me—
the slithery river and hills beyond
and the bluish hills beyond those hills—

pretending to be the kind of English poet
who loved to regard the world from a prospect,
one of whom even had a witty epitaph
engraved on the tombstone of his hound.

LE CHIEN

I remember late one night in Paris
speaking at length to a dog in English
about the future of American culture.

No wonder she kept cocking her head
as I went on about "summer movies"
and the intolerable poetry of my compatriots.

I was standing and she was sitting
on a dim street in front of a butcher shop,
and come to think of it, she could have been waiting

for the early morning return of the lambs
and the bleeding sides of beef
to their hooks in the window.

For my part, I had mixed my drinks,
trading in the tulip of wine
for the sharp nettles of whiskey.

Why else would I be wasting my time
and hers trying to explain "corn dog,"
"white walls," and "March of Dimes"?

She showed such patience for a dog
without breeding while I went on—
in a whisper now after shouts from a window—

about "helmet laws" and "tag sale,"
wishing I had my camera
so I could take a picture of her home with me.

On the loopy way back to my hotel—
after some long and formal goodbyes—
I kept thinking how I would have loved

to hang her picture over the mantle,
where my maternal grandmother
now looks down from her height as always,

silently complaining about the choice of the frame.
Then, before dinner each evening
I could stand before the image of that very dog,

a glass of wine in hand,
submitting all of my troubles and petitions
to the court of her dark-brown, forgiving eyes.

ANOTHER REASON I DON'T KEEP
A GUN IN THE HOUSE

The neighbor's dog will not stop barking.
He is barking the same high, rhythmic bark
that he barks every time they leave the house.
They must switch him on on their way out.

The neighbor's dog will not stop barking.
I close all the windows in the house
and put on a Beethoven symphony full blast
but I can still hear him muffled under the music,
barking, barking, barking,

and now I can see him sitting in the orchestra,
his head raised confidently as if Beethoven
had included a part for barking dog.

When the record finally ends, he is still barking,
sitting there in the oboe section barking,
his eyes fixed on the conductor who is
entreating him with his baton

while the other musicians listen in respectful silence
to the famous barking dog solo,
that endless coda that first established
Beethoven as an innovative genius.

TO A STRANGER BORN IN SOME DISTANT COUNTRY HUNDREDS OF YEARS FROM NOW

> *I write poems for a stranger who will be born in some distant country hundreds of years from now.*
>
> —MARY OLIVER

Nobody here likes a wet dog.
No one wants anything to do with a dog
that is wet from being out in the rain
or retrieving a stick from a lake.
Look how she wanders around the crowded pub tonight
going from one person to another
hoping for a pat on the head, a rub behind the ears,
something that could be given with one hand
without even ruffling the conversation.

But everyone pushes her away,
some with a knee, others with the sole of a boot.
Even the children, who don't realize she is wet
until they go to pet her,
push her away
then wipe their hands on their clothes.
And whenever she heads toward me,
I show her my palm, and she turns aside.

O stranger of the future!
O inconceivable being!
whatever the shape of your house,
however you scoot from place to place,
no matter how strange and colorless the clothes you wear,
I bet nobody there likes a wet dog either.
I bet everybody in your pub,
even the children, pushes her away.

A DOG ON HIS MASTER

As young as I look,
I am growing older faster than he,
seven to one
is the ratio they tend to say.

Whatever the number,
I will pass him one day
and take the lead
the way I do on our walks in the woods.

And if this ever manages
to cross his mind,
it would be the sweetest
shadow I have ever cast on snow or grass.

THE REVENANT

I am the dog you put to sleep,
as you like to call the needle of oblivion,
come back to tell you this simple thing:
I never liked you—not one bit.

When I licked your face,
I thought of biting off your nose.
When I watched you toweling yourself dry,
I wanted to leap and unman you with a snap.

I resented the way you moved,
your lack of animal grace,
the way you would sit in a chair to eat,
a napkin on your lap, knife in your hand.

I would have run away,
but I was too weak, a trick you taught me
while I was learning to sit and heel,
and—greatest of insults—shake hands without a hand.

I admit the sight of the leash
would excite me
but only because it meant I was about
to smell things you had never touched.

You do not want to believe this,
but I have no reason to lie.
I hated the car, the rubber toys,
disliked your friends and, worse, your relatives.

The jingling of my tags drove me mad.
You always scratched me in the wrong place.
All I ever wanted from you
was food and fresh water in my metal bowls.

While you slept, I watched you breathe
as the moon rose in the sky.
It took all of my strength
not to raise my head and howl.

Now I am free of the collar,
the yellow raincoat, monogrammed sweater,
the absurdity of your lawn,
and that is all you need to know about this place

except what you already supposed
and are glad it did not happen sooner—
that everyone here can read and write,
the dogs in poetry, the cats and all the others in prose.

WALKING MY SEVENTY-FIVE-YEAR-OLD DOG

She's painfully slow,
so I often have to stop and wait
while she sniffs some roadside weeds
as if she were reading the biography of a famous dog.

And she's not a pretty sight any more,
dragging one of her hind legs,
her coat too matted to brush or comb,
and a snout white as a marshmallow.

We usually walk down a disused road
that runs along the edge of a lake,
whose surface trembles in a high wind
and is slow to ice over as the months grow cold.

We don't walk very far before
she sits down on her worn haunches
and looks up at me with her rheumy eyes.
Then it's time to carry her back to the car.

Just thinking about the honesty in her eyes,
I realize I should tell you
she's not really seventy-five. She's fourteen.
I guess I was trying to appeal to your sense

of the bizarre, the curiosities of the sideshow.
I mean who really cares about another person's dog?
Everything else I've said is true,
except the part about her being fourteen.

I mean she's old, but not that old,
and it's not nice to divulge the true age of a lady.

THE DAY LASSIE DIED

It is 5:40 in Sawyer County, Wisconsin, a Tuesday
a few days before the birthday of Martin Luther, yes
it is 1959 and I need to do my chores,
which include milking the ten cows—
did I mention it's 5:40 in the morning?—
and driving them with a stick into the pasture.

After breakfast (I am thinking oatmeal
with brown sugar and some raisins)
I will drive the twelve miles into town
and pick up a few things,

a tin of hoof softener for the horse,
some batteries, shells, a pair of rubber gloves,
and something for my wife but I don't know what.
Maybe this cotton apron
with little pictures of the Eiffel Tower on it,

or she might like some hairpins, a box of tissues,
yet I am tempted by this anthology
of the Cavalier poets edited by Thomas Crofts
or maybe *A History of Eton College* by J. W. Hill,

but after pacing up and down the aisles
of Olsen's Emporium, I finally settle on
The Zen Teaching of Huang Po
translated from the Chinese (obviously)
by John Blofeld and published
recently by the infamous Grove Press,

and when I take everything up to Henry
at the big bronze cash register,
he asks have you seen today's *Sentinel*
and there's her face, the dark eyes,
the long near-smile, and the flowing golden coat

and I'm leaning on the barn door back home
while my own collie, who looks a lot like her,
lies curled outside in a sunny patch
and all you can hear as the morning warms up
is the sound of the cows' heavy breathing.

DOG YEARS

Today I turned
420 in dog years,
so I have decided to take myself
for a long walk on the path around the lake,

and when I get back home,
I will jump up on my chest,
lick my nose, ears, and eyelids
while yelling at myself to get down.

And I will replenish my bowl
with cold water from the tap
and hand myself a biscuit from the jar
and accept it gingerly with my teeth.

Then I will make three circles
and lie down under my desk
and fall asleep there
with my chin resting on my paws.

And as I type away all morning,
I will reach down now and then
to stroke my furry, venerable head,
and to make sure I haven't run away.

DOG WITH NO NAME

The night was clear
and the moon was yellow
are such good opening lines
I'm surprised others haven't used them.

But that's the way it was
that night when I noticed
a medium-size dog
crossing my lawn
apparently on his way somewhere.

I was alone for several reasons,
so I tried to get him to come over,
by whistling and barking
then by guessing his name.

I used some common ones
like Butch, Scruffy, and Max,
before going exotic.
"Chaucer!" "Pencil!"
"Pepin the Short!"
I yelled after him from the porch
as he disappeared like a spirit
without a home into a dark hedge.

And that left me to wonder
about his name and who he was
and who I was for that matter,
me in a blue half-buttoned shirt
outside with a tumbler of whiskey
and a moon that was just
as yellow as it was before the dog,

which is when I realized
that like everyone else I was many things,

but now I was the man with cupped hands
who called "Stagger Lee!"
and there he suddenly was,
trotting my way in the moonlight.

GENIUS

was what they called you in high school
if you tripped on a shoelace in the hall
and all your books went flying.

Or if you walked into an open locker door,
you would be known as Einstein,
who imagined riding a streetcar into infinity.

Later, genius became someone
who could take a sliver of chalk and squire pi
a hundred places out beyond the decimal point,

or a man painting on his back on a scaffold,
or drawing a waterwheel in a margin,
or spinning out a little night music.

But earlier this week on a wooded path,
I thought the swans afloat on the reservoir
were the true geniuses,

the ones who had figured out how to fly,
how to be both beautiful and brutal,
and how to mate for life.

Twenty-four geniuses in all,
for I numbered them as Yeats had done,
deployed upon the calm, crystalline surface,

forty-eight if we count their white reflections,
or an even fifty if you want to throw in me
and the dog running up ahead,

who were at least smart enough to be out
that morning—she sniffing the ground,
me with my head up in the bright morning air.

BIOGRAPHICAL NOTES
IN AN ANTHOLOGY OF HAIKU

> *Walking the dog,*
> *you meet*
> *lots of dogs.*
> —*SŌSHI*

One was a seventeenth-century doctor
arrested for trading with Dutch merchants.
One loved *sake* then disappeared
through the doors of a monastery in his final years.

Another was a freight agent
who became a nun after her husband died.
Quite a few lived the samurai life
excelling in the lance, sword, and horseback riding

as well as poetry, painting, and calligraphy.
This one started writing poems at eight,
and that one was a rice merchant of some repute.
One was a farmer, another ran a pharmacy.

But next to the name of my favorite, Sōshi,
there is no information at all,
not even a guess at his years and a question mark,
which left me looking vacantly at the wall

after I had read his perfect little poem.
Whether you poke your nose into Plato
or get serious with Saint John of the Cross,
you will not find a more unassailable truth

than walking the dog, you meet lots of dogs
or a sweeter one, I would add.
If I were a teacher with a student
who deserved punishment, I would make him write

Walking the dog, you meet lots of dogs
on the blackboard a hundred thousand times
or until the boy discovered
that this was no punishment at all, but a treat.

And if I were that student
holding a broken piece of chalk,
every panel filled with my white writing,
I would stand by one of the tall windows

to watch the other students running in the yard
shouting each other's names,
the large autumn trees sheltering their play,
everything so clear now, thanks to the genius of Sōshi.

ALL DRESSED UP

When I leaned over this morning
to get a closer look at the ants
circling the edge of the sink
in the usual ant parade,
I realized they were much too tiny
to slip on a bathrobe,
read a magazine, or wear a wedding ring.

A dog, on the other hand,
will sometimes allow itself to be dressed up
whenever its owner indulges in a bit
of anthropomorphic skylarking.

Yes, the same creature known
to bolt through a screen door
or dig up a bed of petunias with its nose

may sit still on occasion,
playing doctor in a white lab coat
or pose chin-strapped to a birthday hat,
candles dancing in the background.

In Colorado, I once saw a dog in a tuxedo
walk down an aisle and give the bride away.

But dogs are happiest on their own,
stepping on their water bowls,
staring up at the mystery of a closed door,
walking from room to room
before making three circles
like the odd number of flowers in a vase.

And I'm happiest every morning
when my dog steers me
into the kitchen where, as I slowly
open yet another can of his food,

we hold our mutual gaze,
me reading his mind and he reading mine.

THE GUARDIAN

Giovanni Pascoli wrote about this in Italian
before Heaney had a chance
to translate it into English,
so my pencil could wonder about it, too,
a noticing, that is, of the farm dogs
who race barking after every passing cart
or coach, nipping at hooves in a billow of dust.

I've seen such dogs run after a bicycle
or a car, then stop outpaced,
stand still for a moment to make sure
the intruder has given up
any thought of making trouble,
before running back to its post
under a bush or in the shadow of a barn.

Is it madness, this inability to distinguish
between friend or foe, or is it wise
if you can't tell one from the other,
to run barking madly after everyone
simply to be on the safe side?

Whatever the case, it's a kind of job
and you're free to do it all year round.

And in return, this guardian of family
and farm, roosters and hens,
is rewarded with kibble and scraps
and a porch to sleep on when it rains.
And best of all, he is given a name
that is his and his alone,
enough to turn his head and bring him home.

GOOD NEWS

When the news came in over the phone
that you did not have cancer, as they first thought,
I was in the kitchen trying to follow a recipe,
glancing from cookbook to stove,
shifting my glasses from my forehead to my nose,

a recipe, as it turned out, for ratatouille,
a complicated vegetable dish,
which would have any dog turning up his nose.

If you had been here, I imagine
you would be curled up by the door as usual,
sleeping with your head resting on your tail.

Yet after I learned that you were not sick,
everything took on a different look
and appeared to be more itself than it usually is.

For example (and that's the first and last time
I will ever use those words in a poem),
I decided I should grate some cheese,

not even knowing if it was right for ratatouille,
because the sight of the cheese grater
with its red handle lying in the drawer

among the other utensils made me marvel
at how this thing was so perfectly intended
to grate cheese, just as you, with your long smile

and your smooth brown and white coat,
are perfectly designed to be the dog you perfectly are.

SPECIES

I have no need for a biscuit,
a chew toy, or two bowls on the floor.
No desire to investigate a shrub
or sleep on an oval mat by the back door,

but sometimes waiting at a light,
I start to identify with the blond Lab
with his head out the rear window
of the station wagon idling next to me.

And if we speed off together
and I can see his dark lips flapping
in the wind and his eyes closed
then I am sitting in the balcony of envy.

Look at *you*, I usually say
when I pass a terrier on a leash
trotting briskly along as if running
his usual weekday morning errands,

and I stop to stare at any dog
who is peering around a corner,
returning a stick to the thrower,
or just staring back at me from a porch.

So, early this morning
there was no avoiding a twinge
of jealousy for the young spaniel
tied to a bench in the shade

who was now wagging
not just his tail but the whole of himself
to see a woman in a summer dress
emerge from the glass doors of the post office.

She then crouched down in front of him,
taking his chin in her hand,
and said in a mock-scolding tone
"I told you I'd be right back, silly,"

leaving the dog to sit down
and return her gaze with a look
of understanding which seemed to say
"I know. I know. I never doubted that you would."

TWO CREATURES

The last time I looked, the dog was lying
on the freshly cut grass
but now she has moved under the picnic table.

I wonder what causes her to shift
from one place to another,
to get up for no apparent reason from her spot

by the stove, scratch one ear,
then relocate, slumping down
on the other side of the room by the big window,

or I will see her hop onto the couch to nap
then later find her down
on the Turkish carpet, her nose in the fringe.

The moon rolls across the night sky
and stops to peer down at the earth,
and the dog rolls through these rooms

and onto the lawn, pausing here and there
to sleep or to stare up at me, head in her paws,
to consider the scentless pen in my hand

or the open book on my lap.
And because her eyes always follow me
maybe she wonders, too, why I

shift from place to place,
from the couch to the sink
or the pencil sharpener on the wall—

two creatures bound by wonderment
though unlike her, I have never worried
after letting her out the back door

that she might zoom off in the car again,
but this time, never to return
to stroke my head or fill my bowl with water.

MAGICAL REALISM

It's a rainy Saturday night in London
and many of the male dogs
have gathered at their favorite pub,
the Ball and Stick,
where they lower their heads
to drink from their bowls of ale,
for this is not an off-the-wall cartoon,
where they would be standing at the bar
holding a pint glass impossibly in one paw.

No, this is just a bit of fiction,
but not by a South American fantasist,
where many strange things are done.
And that's why the dogs are not
smoking cigars or playing darts,
or gossiping about their owners.
Nor is there any laughter, no sports on the telly,
no back-slapping, which would require
standing up all night on your hind legs.

And that's also why it's so quiet
for a Saturday night with your mates,
unlike the clamor down the lane
at the Axe and Hammer,
or around the corner at the King's Piston.
Here, it's just the low sounds of lapping
and a round of barking each time
a new dog happens to walk in the door,
yes, on all fours and without a stitch of clothes.

THE COLLAR

A dog's collar
typically features
a silvery D-ring
where the leash
is clipped on,
and usually
the pendants
of a gray rabies tag
and a smaller ID
bearing a number
and his name,
which can work
to unhinge your heart
when the collar
is slipped,
over his ears
and off his body,
freeing him for good.

TRYING TO WRITE A DOG POEM
IN A HOUSE WITH TWO CATS

From a couch
littered with throw pillows

they are staring at me
and my open notebook,

and even though their tails
are not twitching

and their secret inboard
motors are not audible,

I know they are assuming
in unison

that I am writing
yet another dog poem

rather than one about
the two of them,

but as you can see,
they are actually

featured here,
an irony which is all

I have to compete
with their ceaseless gaze.

YOUR POEM

The choice of season is up to you,
though winter is best for poetry,
and you can pick any time of day—
not just my favorites, dawn or late afternoon,
and, if you like, mention the day of the week.

What emotion is being expressed
I leave up to you as well—
buoyant ease in the shadow of mortality
being one of many options, the mixing
of the sugar of joy and the salt of sorrow another.

Whether the poet is standing, sitting,
or supine, I also place in your hands.

Where we are located is another matter.
You're in charge now. Entirely your call.
The choices here can be overwhelming
in a world of at least 10,000 places,
so don't hurry your selection with this one.

Train windows and rooftops are good.
Or you could pick a beach scene,
a solitary swimmer, arm bent above a wave.
Toss in some shells, whatever you think works.
The pen is in your hand.
You're up there in the driver's seat.

I'm not even here anymore.
I'm somewhere else,
leaning against a tree, as it happens.
It's a Monday around dusk.
Lots of yellow leaves float down.
I'm 27. A dog stretching at my side.

AS TIME GOES BY

Like the dog who forgot
where he buried his bone

the old farmer forgot
where he buried the dog.

THE FOLLOWING DOGS

There are dogs who will follow you
perpetually and as gladly
as if it were their purpose in life,
at least while in the act of following you.

Other dogs enjoy being followed.
They sniff around, look back, then run ahead.

W. B. Yeats, so monumentally heartsick,
spent his boyhood summers
following a black dog and a white dog
around the hilly Irish countryside,
as if that were the purpose of his life,
which it might have been at the time.

Clearly, there are worse practices
than spending your time following a dog
whichever way she may roam
into the woods or across a stream.

How would it be possible
to slap a child or smuggle arms
to a band of wrathful guerrillas
if you're busy keeping up with a dog?

So, instead of following your bliss,
follow around some lighthearted dog.

Surely, it's better than doing nothing,
if anything *were* better than doing nothing,

which, setting dogs aside for now,
is said to be the best thing one can do
or not do, but in a positive way, forever, amen.

ACKNOWLEDGMENTS

We are deeply indebted to our editor David Ebershoff and agent Chris Calhoun for bringing this book into being.

My thanks to the editors of *The New Yorker* and *Five Points* for publishing "All Dressed Up" and "The Guardian," respectively.

ABOUT THE AUTHOR

BILLY COLLINS is the author of fifteen collections of poetry, the most recent being *Water, Water*. He is a former Distinguished Professor of English at Lehman College (CUNY). He served as United States Poet Laureate and as New York State Poet. He is a New York Public Library "Literary Lion" and a member of the American Academy of Arts and Letters. He is currently "between dogs," his most recent one being an Australian shepherd mix named Jeannine. He lives in Winter Park, Florida, with his wife, Suzannah.

Facebook.com/BillyCollinsPoetry
Instagram: @the_real_billy_collins / @pamelasztybel

ABOUT THE ARTIST

PAMELA SZTYBEL is a painter who divides her time between New York City and Bridgewater, Connecticut. She has a dog named Jack.

ABOUT THE TYPE

This book was set in Caslon, a typeface first designed in 1722 by William Caslon (1692–1766). Its widespread use by most English printers in the early eighteenth century soon supplanted the Dutch typefaces that had formerly prevailed. The roman is considered a "workhorse" typeface due to its pleasant, open appearance, while the italic is exceedingly decorative.